EXPLORE
POETRY!

Andi Diehn

Illustrated by Bryan Stone

Newest titles in the **Explore Your World!** Series

Nomad Press
A division of Nomad Communications
10 9 8 7 6 5 4 3 2 1

This book was manufactured by Marquis Book Printing,
Montmagny Québec, Canada
April 2015, Job #109672

ISBN Softcover: 978-1-61930-283-9
ISBN Hardcover: 978-1-61930-279-2

Illustrations by Bryan Stone
Educational Consultant, Marla Conn

Questions regarding the ordering of this book should be addressed to
Nomad Press
2456 Christian St.
White River Junction, VT 05001
www.nomadpress.net

Printed in Canada.

CONTENTS

Interested in primary sources? Look for this icon.
Use a smartphone or tablet app to scan the QR code and explore more about poetry! You can find a list of URLs on the Resources page.

POEM!

Twinkle, twinkle, little star,
How I wonder what you are.
Up above the world so high,
Like a diamond in the sky.
Twinkle, twinkle, little star,
How I wonder what you are.

Words to Know

nursery rhyme: a short poem or song for children that often tells a story.

poem: a piece of writing that describes an event, idea, or emotion in a vivid way.

What happens when you read these words? Many of you will set the words to a tune without even thinking about it. *Twinkle, Twinkle, Little Star* is a popular **nursery rhyme** that might have been sung to you when you were a baby. You know what else it is? A **poem**!

Words to Know

pattern: a way of arranging words in a design to create meaning.

poetry: the writings of a poet.

Poems are words written in a **pattern**. Have you ever done a jigsaw puzzle? You take all the pieces and move them around and fit them together. Then you have a picture that tells a story.

Maybe your jigsaw puzzle picture is of two puppies playing in the grass. All of those pieces of cardboard came together to tell a story about those two puppies.

The word *poem* comes from the Ancient Greek word *poema*, which means "that which was made."

Poetry is just like that. The words are like the puzzle pieces. You move the words around and fit them together until you have a poem. A poem is like a picture because it tells a story. In *Twinkle, Twinkle, Little Star*, we find a story about someone wondering what stars are. Poems are words put together in patterns that tell stories, teach lessons, or describe people, places, or things.

In this poem we find a story about a girl who lives in a kingdom by the sea.

POEM!

Annabel Lee by Edgar Allan Poe

It was many and many a year ago,
In a kingdom by the sea,
That a maiden there lived
 whom you may know
By the name of ANNABEL LEE;
And this maiden she lived with no other thought
Than to love and be loved by me.

Words to Know

poet: a person who writes poems.

rhyming: when words sound alike except for the first letter.

context: the background or setting of a poem.

KNOW YOUR POETS: ROALD DAHL

Have you ever read the book *Charlie and the Chocolate Factory*, or seen the movie *Matilda*? Roald Dahl (1916–1990) is a famous children's book author and **poet** from England. In addition to books and short stories, he also wrote poetry, which was often dark and scary.

You can listen to Roald Dahl read his own poetry. How does the **rhyming** make the poem sound? Do the rhymes sound like Dahl came up with them easily? Are there any words you don't know? Can you figure them out according to the **context**, or the surrounding words? The title of the poem might be familiar, but the poem tells a very different story than the one you might have heard before. Why do you think Dahl did this?

ROALD DAHL

PS

Listen to Roald Dahl read his own poetry.

THE FIRST POEMS

The very first poems were spoken or sung out loud. **Scholars** believe that poetry came before writing. People memorized the poems and told them to each other without ever writing them down. One the earliest of these told-aloud poems is called *The Tale of the Shipwrecked Sailor*. Historians think this poem was created in **ancient** Egypt around 2500 **BCE**. That's more than 4,500 years ago!

Another ancient poem, called *The Vedas*, is made up of four poems. The oldest of these poems was **composed** around 1500 BCE. *The Vedas* is very important to people who practice **Hinduism**, many of whom believe God wrote the poems.

Have you ever heard of *The Odyssey*? This is an ancient, very long poem called an **epic** that is still read today.

Words to Know

scholar: a person who studies a subject for a long time and knows a lot about it.

ancient: from a long time ago.

BCE: put after a date, BCE stands for Before Common Era and counts down to zero. CE stands for Common Era and counts up from zero. These non-religious terms correspond to BC and AD. This book was printed in 2015 CE.

compose: to write.

Hinduism: the main **religion** of India. It includes the worship of many gods and the belief that after death you return in a different form.

religion: a set of beliefs.

epic: a long poem, usually about the life of a hero or heroine.

ANCIENT POETRY

Some ancient poems use words that are much different from those we use today. Are any of the words in these ancient poems new to you? What do you think they mean? Look in the glossary at the back of the book to check your answers.

The Vedas

Sing with new lauds his
   exploits wrought aforetime,
   the deeds of him, yea, him
   who moveth swiftly,

When, hurling forth his weapons
   in the battle, he with impetuous
   wrath lays low the foemen.

The Odyssey

And when long years and seasons

wheeling brought around that point of time

ordained for him to make his
   passage homeward,

trials and dangers, even so, attended him

even in Ithaca, near those he loved.

Words to Know

hero: a person who can do things that seem impossible.

mythological: having to do with a myth, which is an ancient story that may or may not be true.

siren: an imaginary woman whose singing made sailors crash their ships.

recite: to speak a poem or other story out loud.

The Odyssey tells of the journey of Odysseus, an ancient Greek **hero**, traveling home to his wife and son. Odysseus had been at war for 10 years and it takes him another 10 to get home!

This epic contains **mythological** creatures, such as the one-eyed Cyclops and the beautiful, deadly **sirens**. A blind poet named Homer is credited with making up *The Odyssey* and traveling around ancient Greece **reciting** it. Just like today, people back then loved to hear about magical creatures, heroes, and journeys. Why do you think we like these kinds of tales?

5

Words to Know

civilization: a community of people that is advanced in art, science, and government.

rhythm: a regular pattern of **beats**.

beat: the rhythmic sound in a line of poetry or music.

phase: a period of development.

generation: all the people born around the same time.

imagination: the ability to think of something new.

emotion: a strong feeling about something or someone.

characteristic: a feature of a person, place, or thing.

Where does poetry come from?

JUST 4 FUN

Poet-trees!

Poetry was a way for people to pass along stories about individuals, families, religions, and even entire **civilizations**. Because poetry has **rhythm**, the lines are easier for our brains to remember than stories. Sometimes poetry was set to music to make it even easier to remember.

Did you Know?

Poetry has gone through many different **phases** since *The Vedas* and *The Odyssey*.

Many **generations** all over the world have come up with their own styles of poetry. Romantic poetry, written in the late 1700s and early 1800s, focused on **imagination** and **emotion**. Beat poetry, written in the 1940s and 1950s, was known for trying different things.

Even as poems change their shape and their reasons for existing, they share important **characteristics** with other styles of poems. We'll learn about some of these characteristics later in the book.

POETRY TODAY

Is it strange to think about singing and reciting information in order to remember it? We don't need to do that today because we have easy ways to **access** the information we need. Smart phones and laptops help us keep track of lots of different things!

Words to Know

access: the ability to use or get something.

publish: to produce work for the public.

anthology: a collection of poems by different authors.

literary journal: a magazine in which poems and stories are published for a small, interested group.

Poetry is also an art form. It's beautiful to read and listen to. People feel good when they read poetry, and some studies show that poetry is even healthy for our bodies.

These days, poets such as Homer no longer travel the world reciting poetry. People share poetry in different ways. The Internet is a good place to post poems. Some authors **publish** whole books of their poetry. Poems can also be collected in books called **anthologies**, which contain poems from many different writers. Magazines, newspapers, newsletters, and **literary journals** contain lots of poetry published by both beginner poets and experienced poets.

Poetry is also read out loud, just like in Homer's time. Libraries, bookstores, and coffee shops host **poetry slams** for people who want to read their poems out loud in front of an **audience**. You can hear spoken word poetry over the radio and on the Internet. Maybe your classroom will host a poetry reading and you can hear what your classmates have been working on.

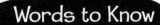

Words to Know

poetry slam: a competition where people perform their poetry for a group of people.

audience: a group of people who gather to listen to or watch something.

literary form: a form of writing, such as a story, novel, or poem.

inspiration: something that gives people ideas.

draft: one of several versions of a written piece of work.

Did you Know?

The first poetry slam took place in Chicago in 1984. Now poetry slams can be found in cities all over the world!

For thousands of years, poetry has been inviting listeners to think, feel, and experience the world in different ways. Many poems are easy to read and understand. And many forms of poetry are very easy to write. Poetry is a **literary form** that everyone can take part in. Let's see what poems you find inside yourself!

MAKE A POETRY JOURNAL

Most poets carry a notebook around with them wherever they go. Why? In case they think of something when they're not at their desks! **Inspiration** can happen at any moment, and it's a great idea to keep all of your poetry thoughts and **drafts** in one place.

SUPPLIES

- ℓ 4 pieces of blank paper
- ℓ stapler
- ℓ scissors
- ℓ ruler
- ℓ empty cereal box or other thin cardboard
- ℓ glue
- ℓ markers

1 Fold each sheet of paper in half twice. What you have now are called signatures.

2 Nest the four signatures so their spines are all touching.

ONE SIGNATURE

FOUR SIGNATURES

3 Staple along the spine. Carefully cut along the folded edges so every page is loose.

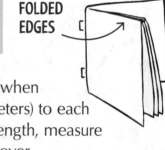

FOLDED EDGES

4 Measure the width and length of your book when it is open and flat. Add a quarter inch (6 millimeters) to each measurement. Following your new width and length, measure and cut out your cardboard. This will be your cover.

5 Fold the cover in half and glue it to the outside pages of your book. When it's dry, decorate your cover so it's an original! Write a title and your name. You can also number your pages, if you want. These homemade books are small, so they might fill up fast. Make new ones whenever you need to.

Poetry Journal!

FORMS OF POETRY

There are lots of different types of poetry, just as there are different kinds of songs and artwork. Poems can be long or short, they can rhyme or not rhyme, or they can make a certain shape on the page. Some poetry requires counting and other poetry follows no rules at all.

You might find that you like some types of poetry more than others. Not everyone likes heavy metal music or classical music or reggae—and not everyone likes **limericks** or **haiku**.

Words to Know

limerick: a rhyming poem made up of five lines. The first, second, and fifth lines rhyme with each other, and the third and fourth lines rhyme with each other.

haiku: a short, simple poem that usually has 17 **syllables**.

syllable: the separate sounds in a word.

Poetry is a kind of writing that is very **accessible**. Anyone can read it, write it, and find something interesting about it. **Here are some of the more popular forms of poetry.**

ACROSTIC POEMS

Acrostic poems are very simple poems that can spark some very deep thinking. **What do you notice about this poem?**

POEM!

Susie

Sushi for dinner

Umbrellas on rainy days

Surprises on my birthday

Intelligent conversation

Extra sunny summer days

Words to Know

accessible: able to be read and understood by many people.

acrostic poem: a poem where certain letters in each line spell out a word or phrase.

phrase: a group of two or more words that **express** an idea but do not form a complete sentence.

express: to talk or write about or show in some way something you are thinking or feeling.

A double acrostic makes words out of the letters at the beginning and the end of each line.

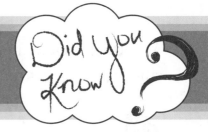

To write an acrostic poem, you start with one word and think of a word or **phrase** for each letter in the word. Many people use their names as their starting word. Another idea is to use the name of the town you live in, your dog's name, your favorite color, or your favorite movie star. The fun thing about acrostic poems is that there are no limits on subject matter!

Words to Know

found poem: a poem made up of words found in other writings.

collage: a work of art made up of different pieces of material.

image: a picture of something.

The lines you write for each letter should have something to do with your subject. If you're writing an acrostic poem about your dog, every line needs to be about your dog.

FOUND POEMS

A **found poem** might seem like a very easy poem to write, since the words are already there in front of you! But poetry is all about making patterns. The important part of writing a found poem is to put your found words into a pattern that has meaning.

Have you ever made a **collage** out of photographs cut from magazines? The collage you end up with is very different from the individual **images** you start with.

You might choose pictures that **represent** things that you like to eat, places you wish to visit, or instruments you want to learn to play. By choosing those pictures and arranging them on a poster, you create a collage with a very **specific** meaning.

Poets can create very different patterns using the same words, just as artists can create very different paintings using the same colors.

Did you know?

A found poem is similar to a collage. To write a found poem, poets choose words from books, magazines, newspapers, websites, letters—anything that has words. Some poets use the labels found on packages of cookies. You can even write a found poem using whole phrases from a book or even all the words of a road sign. Where do you think the words in this found poem came from?

POEM!

Complex, flowering poetry
Lives between syllables
And starts action with brains.

Words to Know

text: the words in a piece of writing.

Why do found poems sound and feel so different from the **text** they were found in? Remember, poetry is interesting and beautiful because of the patterns the poet creates with words.

KNOW YOUR POETS: WILLIAM SHAKESPEARE

Shakespeare (1564–1616), who lived in England, is famous for writing plays and poems. A poet living today named Jen Bervin created found poems from Shakespeare's poems. How are Bervin's poems different from Shakespeare's poems? Do you think Shakespeare would like her poems?

WILLIAM SHAKESPEARE

PS You can see Jen Bervin's found poems here.

LIMERICKS

The poems we've learned about so far don't rhyme and don't follow a lot of rules. Rhyming poetry can be harder to write because there are more parts to pay attention to. There are rules to follow about which words rhyme, and some rhyming poetry requires a certain number of beats in every line.

How do you know when words rhyme? Rhyming words sound the same except for their first sound. *Cat, mat, bat, rat, fat*—these words all rhyme. Two words that rhyme exactly, such as *dock* and *clock*, are called a **perfect rhyme**.

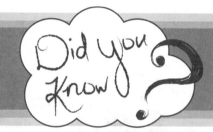

Words to Know

perfect rhyme: words that have the same ending sound.

slant rhyme: words that almost rhyme, such as *one* and *down*.

What about *spider* and *beside her*? In poetry, this would be considered a rhyme, even though the words don't follow the rules for rhyming. Do *one* and *down* rhyme with each other? Not quite, but almost. These are called **slant rhymes**.

No one is certain why limericks are called limericks, but most people think the name comes from the Irish city of Limerick.

Did you Know?

A limerick is an example of rhyming poetry. It is made up of five lines, with the first, second, and fifth lines rhyming with each other, and the third and fourth lines rhyming with each other. In the nursery rhyme below, *dock, clock,* and *dock* rhyme, while *one* and *down* rhyme.

Hickory, Dickory, Dock

Hickory, dickory, dock
The mouse ran up the clock.   RHYME
The clock struck one,
The mouse ran down,   RHYME
Hickory, dickory, dock.

15

Words to Know

emphasize: to give special importance to something.

Each line in a limerick has a certain beat. Let's read the nursery rhyme again and this time **emphasize** the beats. Clap your hands as you read the poem out loud.

POEM!

HICKory, **DICK**ory, **DOCK**
The **MOUSE** ran **UP** the **CLOCK**.
The **CLOCK** struck **ONE**,
The **MOUSE** ran **DOWN**,
HICKory, **DICK**ory, **DOCK**.

Every limerick carries a close variation of this beat. Limericks are also often funny and silly.

POEM!

JUST **4** FUN

There was an Old Man with a beard
Who said, "It is just as I feared!
Two owls and a hen,
Four larks and a wren,
Have all built their nests in my beard!"

HAIKU

Haiku poems are sometimes simpler to read and write than other poems. This is partly because they are so short—just three lines! But haiku follow certain rules. Haiku poems almost always have 17 syllables—five on the first line, seven on the second line, and five on the third line.

16

SYLLABLES AND BEATS

Syllables are different than beats. In the previous section on limericks, we counted three beats in a line that contained seven syllables:

HICKory, **DICK**ory, **DOCK**

The beats are where the emphasis falls in a string of words. Syllables are the parts of every word that you hear when it's spoken out loud:

hick-or-y, dick-or-y, dock

Can you hear the difference? This line has three beats and seven syllables.

Haiku are one of the oldest forms of written poetry. An early, longer form of Haiku was first developed in Japan between 700 and 1100 CE. A poet named Matsuo Basho, who lived between 1644 and 1694, refined that early form to the shorter version we know today.

POEM!

Will we meet again
Here at your flowering grave -
Two white butterflies?

Words to Know

simplicity: easy to read and understand.

Basho thought haiku should focus on the simple beauty of nature. While most haiku poems no longer follow Basho's ideas on simple beauty, there is a **simplicity** to poems with only three lines.

Words to Know

shape poem: a poem that forms a shape on the paper.

free verse: a poem that doesn't rhyme or follow a regular structure.

SHAPE POEMS

Some poems aren't happy to live in regular rows. **Shape poems** tell stories not only through the words chosen by the poet but also through the shape the poem makes on the page.

POEM!

If this poem didn't make the shape of a tree, would it be as interesting and as fun to read? Would it have the same meaning if the words were lying straight on the page? Maybe not!

Some shape poems use rhyming words and some use a regular beat. But often the shape poem is **free verse,** which means it doesn't rhyme or follow a regular structure. Usually, the poet finds a shape first and then applies words to it. The shape might be the inspiration for the poem.

The words and the shape work together to accomplish the poet's goals.

WORDS IN THE CLOUDS

Have you ever seen a word cloud? Look at the page across from page 1 to see a word cloud made from the vocabulary words in this book. Can you spot the shape? Word clouds are related to shape poems. You can write a paragraph about any topic you choose and then arrange your words in a shape that's related to your topic. The most important words can be biggest and less important words can be smaller.

You can make your own word clouds at this website.

There are hundreds of different forms of poems to read and write. Some forms are very **structured**. Other forms are more accessible and easy to understand.

Different forms of poetry offer different, interesting ways to express yourself. You might find that you become more **creative** when faced with writing a more **complex** poem, such as a limerick. What happens if you stick with the easier forms, such as haiku?

Words to Know

structured: formed with rules and guidelines.

creative: using imagination to come up with new ideas or things.

complex: the opposite of simple.

How does a poet sneeze?

JUST 4 FUN

Haiku!

FIND A POEM!

Found poems are just waiting to be discovered everywhere you look. There are lots of different ways to create a found poem. With this activity you'll end up with both a poem and a piece of art! If you use a page from a book, make sure it's a book nobody wants anymore.

1 Read over your page of text a couple of times. With your pencil, lightly circle words that you like. Don't think too hard about trying to create a poem! Let your brain find words without too much thought.

2 Paint over everything else on the page except those circled words. Try and paint close to the words to cover your pencil marks. It's okay if the other words peek through the paint.

3 Circle the words in your found poem with your markers and decorate over the paint. You might want to rewrite your poem somewhere on the page. Keep the words in the order they appear on the page!

SUPPLIES

- ℓ Poetry Journal
- ℓ page from a magazine, newspaper, or old book
- ℓ pencil
- ℓ paint and paintbrush
- ℓ markers, glitter glue, stickers
- ℓ cardboard

Great places to find text to cut up, black out, or copy over include recycling bins, used bookstores, and thrift stores that sell boxes of old posters and magazines.

Did you Know?

4 Measure and cut the cardboard so that your page is centered with a frame of cardboard showing on each side. Paint your cardboard a dark color and glue your page to it when everything is dry.

5 Write your found poem in your Poetry Journal and hang your artwork on your wall!

THINK ABOUT IT: When you read your poem in your Poetry Journal, does it feel the same as when you read it from your artwork? How is it different?

Words to Know

tone: the mood of something.

KNOW YOUR POETS: ROBERT FROST

Robert Frost (1874–1963) was an American twentieth century poet who was inspired by the natural world. His poems are often about trees, stone walls, storms, and pastures. One of his poems, titled *The Road Not Taken*, is about a traveller who has to decide between two paths in the forest. Do you think the narrator regrets his decision? Why or why not? What is the **tone** of the poem? Which words are clues to the tone?

 Read *The Road Not Taken* by Robert Frost.

Watch a video of Robert Frost reading another of his poems, *Stopping by Woods on a Snowy Evening*.

ROBERT FROST

HAIKU, LOW COO

Haiku are very short, but they can also be hard to write. Shorter isn't always easier! Try writing your own haiku about something in nature.

SUPPLIES

- ℓ outdoor spot
- ℓ timer
- ℓ pencil
- ℓ paper
- ℓ Poetry Journal

1 Bring your pencil and paper outside and find a spot to sit. Make sure you're comfortable enough to sit still for five minutes!

2 Set the timer for five minutes. Close your eyes and focus your senses on the world around you. What do you hear? What do you feel? Is there a storm coming? Are animals rustling in the leaves at your feet? Do you feel a breeze? The sun?

3 When five minutes have gone by, open your eyes and right away right down a list of things you noticed. These could be words about how you felt, what you heard, or things that were happening around you. Don't think about what your words mean or if they are the best ones to use in a poem. This is your time to **brainstorm**!

Words to Know

brainstorm: to think creatively and without judgment.

4 When you have a list of seven or eight words, choose one or two that are the most interesting. Perhaps you heard a chipmunk in the leaves while you sat. Maybe there was noise from the wind around you. Using those words, write three lines of description. Don't worry about the number of syllables yet! Just get your ideas down on paper.

Basho felt that haiku should be simple, spontaneous, and focused on seeing beauty in ordinary, everyday life.

5 When you have three lines of poetry, count the number of syllables on each line. Remember, haiku often have a syllable pattern of 5, 7, 5.

Syllables by line	Example by Matsuo Basho
5	An old silent pond . . .
7	A frog jumps into the pond,
5	splash! Silence again.

6 Your first draft will probably have too many syllables. Try cutting out words such as *the*, *a*, and *an*. Are there other words you don't need? Is there a shorter word you can use to replace a longer word? Some haiku are more like lists of words about a subject.

7 When you have the right pattern, copy over your final poem on a clean sheet in your Poetry Journal.

THINK ABOUT IT: What words did you choose to describe the sensation of sitting in nature? Do you think someone else reading your haiku would know what you were feeling when you wrote it?

IDEA ROCKS ROCK!

Sometimes it can be hard to feel inspired to write a poem. Maybe you can't think of anything to write about! Give yourself the gift of future ideas by making a set of idea rocks.

SUPPLIES

- ℓ 12–15 small, smooth rocks
- ℓ markers
- ℓ small bag or box

1 Wash and dry each of your rocks.

2 Use your markers to write one word or draw a picture of one object on each rock. To get ideas for your rocks, take a walk around your house and yard. Anything you see—trees, your bed, windows, birds, pets, brothers, sisters, and dirt—can be put on a rock.

3 When you have put an idea on each rock, put them in your bag.

4 When you are stuck for an idea for a poem, reach into your bag and pull out an idea rock. No peeking! Even if you don't want to write a poem about that exact thing, it might spark an idea for a different subject. If you get tired of using those same ideas, you can make a new set of idea rocks.

TRY THIS! Make two bags of idea rocks. Without looking, pull two rocks from each bag and arrange the words to write a found poem!

WHAT'S IN A NAME?

Acrostic poems can be fairly easy to write. They can also reveal some interesting things about yourself!

SUPPLIES

ℓ pencil
ℓ paper
ℓ Poetry Journal

1 Write your name with the letters as a column on the paper, like the example here.

A
L
L
I
S
O
N

2 Starting with the first letter, write a list of things about yourself that start with that letter. These can be **adjectives**, **nouns**, or **verbs**. You might also write a phrase instead of one word. Write two or three words or phrases for each of the letters in your name.

3 Start with a new piece of paper. Choose one word or phrase for each of the letters in your name. Add that word or phrase next to the correct letter so it appears on the same row. Do you need to make any **revisions**? Could you use a different word that would sound better and still mean the same thing?

4 When your poem is finished, copy it into your Poetry Journal.

Active
Laughing
Learning
I
S
O
N

Words to Know

adjective: one of the parts of speech. An adjective is a word, such as *green* or *tall*, that describes a noun.

noun: one of the parts of speech. A noun is a word that is the name of something, such as a person, place, or thing.

verb: one of the parts of speech. A verb is a word, such as *jump* or *see*, that describes an action.

revision: making a change in something to improve it.

MAGNETIC POETRY KIT

Magnetic poetry kits are fun, and you can make your own. These are great for writing found poetry on your refrigerator!

CAUTION: Ask an adult to help you use the knife.

SUPPLIES

- ℓ magnetic paper
- ℓ thin marker
- ℓ craft knife
- ℓ foam pad or piece of wood

1 Write four columns of words on your magnetic paper, or print a list onto the paper from a computer. You can come up with your own words or use a list of the most common English words found here.

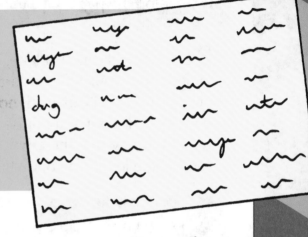

2 With an adult's help, use the craft knife to cut each word out. Make sure you are cutting over a foam pad or wood so that you don't scratch the surface underneath.

3 Now you have your own set of magnetic poetry! Find a plastic bag or a box to keep your poetry pieces in so they don't get lost when you aren't using them!

You can also play with magnetic poetry online!

SUPPLIES

ℓ magnetic
  poetry words
ℓ refrigerator or
  cookie sheet

MAKE MAGNETIC POEMS

When you have the words at your fingertips, poems can be easy and fun to write! Try writing some poems by yourself and with friends using your magnetic poetry kit. Here are a few tips to get started.

1 Without looking, select a bunch of words and stick them on the refrigerator or metal cookie sheet. Arrange them in a way that makes a poem. Rearrange them to make another poem. And do it again a third time! Can you make poems that are very different from each other using the same words?

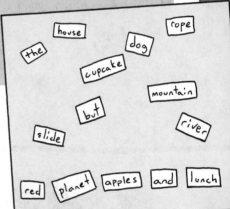

2 Write a poem with a friend. Pick a magnetic word as the first word of the poem. Have your friend pick a different word for the second word of the poem. Go back and forth until you have a complete poem.

3 Use your magnetic words to write the first line of a poem while a friend writes the second line at the same time. When you're both done, put the lines together. Do they make sense? Do they surprise you?

4 Make a poem with your eyes closed. Open your eyes and read it out loud.

THINK ABOUT IT: Words in a poem don't have to follow each other in rows! Try making different shapes with your magnet words. What shapes go well with the subject of your poem?

LITERARY TECHNIQUES

THE FOG COMES
ON LITTLE CAT FEET.

When you read a poem, you might not be thinking about why different lines make you think or feel different ways. You might just be enjoying the language and the pictures it brings to your mind. The poet, however, thought hard about how to tell the story inside the poem.

Poets use **literary techniques** in their poems to **convey** scenes and emotions. Literary techniques are different methods of grouping words to give a poem meaning. **Here are some of the more popular literary techniques you'll find in poetry.**

METAPHOR

A **metaphor** is a way of describing something by saying it's something else.

POEM!

Fog by Carl Sandburg
The fog comes
on little cat feet.
It sits looking
over harbor and city
on silent **haunches**
and then moves on.

Words to Know

metaphor: a way to describe something by saying it is something else.

haunches: the part of the body above the hip.

vaporous: having no solid shape.

stealthy: quiet, sneaky.

Does fog really have cat feet? Does fog sit or look? Does it have haunches? No. Fog is **vaporous**. It doesn't have feet or haunches, and it has no body or eyes so it can't sit or look.

But when Carl Sandburg describes the fog as though it were a cat, he makes readers see fog as something silent, **stealthy**, and alive. The poet has linked two unrelated objects together to encourage readers to stretch their brains and think about things in different ways.

Hey! Talking about a brain stretching is a metaphor! Brains don't really stretch, do they? All different kinds of writing, not just poetry, contain literary techniques.

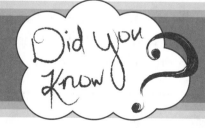
Did you Know?

29

You can find metaphors in lots of different places. Advertisers often use metaphors in slogans. *Taste the rainbow. They're magically delicious! Kellogg's Frosted Flakes brings out the tiger in you!* If you eat Kellogg's Frosted Flakes, you don't actually turn into a tiger, but it's a fun image to think about. It might encourage you to ask your parents to buy that kind of cereal.

MUNCH MUNCH MUNCH

Words to Know

dynamic: active or changing, showing a lot of energy or motion.

When you use metaphors in your own poetry, try to come up with **dynamic** images that will surprise readers. You want your readers to take notice of your words.

MIXING METAPHORS

Sometimes metaphors get confusing—these are called mixed metaphors. What do you think this means: "Her artwork was a clear summer day that marched across the page and shook mud all over the table." This sentence compares a piece of art to three different metaphors that all talk about different subjects. Artwork can either be a summer day, or it can march across the page, or it can shake mud all over the table, but it can't do all three at once. Mixed metaphors are hard to understand and confusing. Good metaphors make a piece of writing much less confusing.

SIMILE

Similes are similar to metaphors, but they always use the words *like* or *as*.

Easter by Joyce Kilmer
The air is like a butterfly
With frail blue wings.
The happy earth looks at the sky
And sings.

POEM!

Words to Know

simile: a figure of speech that compares two different things using the words *like* or *as*.

cliché: a phrase that is used so often it has lost much of its meaning.

The first line of this poem contains a simile: "The air is like a butterfly . . ." The poet is comparing two separate things, the air and a butterfly, and linking them with the word *like*.

If the word *like* was missing and the line was "The air is a butterfly . . ." what literary technique would that be?

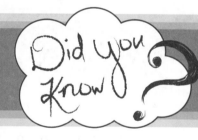

People use similes often in everyday spoken language. Have you ever heard the expression, "as strong as an ox?" Or "as cool as a cucumber?" These are similes. These similes are also called **clichés**. The phrases have been used so often they don't suprise us and we no longer notice them. They almost have no meaning.

When writing your own similes, try to avoid clichés. Think of similes and metaphors as opportunities to make your poem fresh and exciting.

PERSONIFICATION

Personification gives human or animal qualities and characteristics to objects, or human characteristics to animals.

Words to Know

personification: to imagine that an object has human or animal characteristics or that an animal has human characteristics.

POEM!

Hey Diddle Diddle

Hey diddle diddle,
The cat and the fiddle,
The cow jumped over the moon;
The little dog laughed
To see such sport,
And the dish ran away with the spoon.

Did you Know?

Animated movies use lots of personification. What is being personified in *Cars*? *Toy Story*? *Madagascar*?

What is a simile?

JUST 4 FUN

It's like a metaphor!

Can little dogs really laugh? Can dishes and spoons run away? Little dogs might yip and seem like they're laughing, but they can't laugh the way humans do. And dishes and spoons never move unless someone else moves them. The little dog, the dish, and the spoon are all examples of personification.

What if the poem read like this? "The little dog made yipping noises and shook its belly as though it found the cow very funny." It doesn't have the same **concise** feel to it. It takes many more words and leaves the readers with images that aren't as easy to picture.

Remember, in poems, every word matters. Literary techniques such as personification help keep the word count of a poem low and every word important.

Words to Know

concise: giving a lot of information in a few, clear words.

hyperbole: an exaggerated description.

exaggeration: to say something is much more than it really is.

HYPERBOLE HYPE

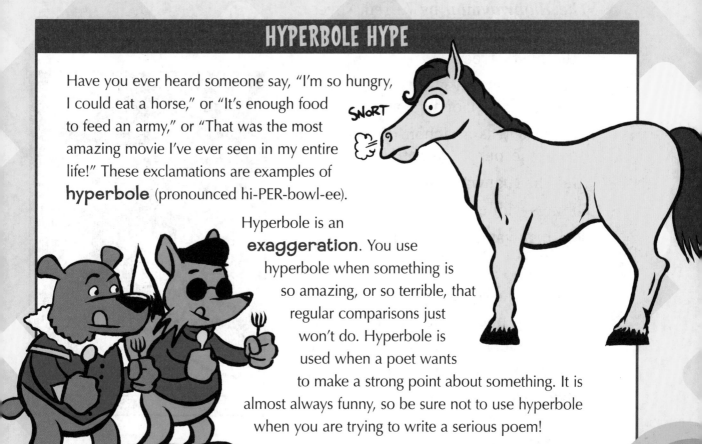

Have you ever heard someone say, "I'm so hungry, I could eat a horse," or "It's enough food to feed an army," or "That was the most amazing movie I've ever seen in my entire life!" These exclamations are examples of **hyperbole** (pronounced hi-PER-bowl-ee).

SNORT

Hyperbole is an **exaggeration**. You use hyperbole when something is so amazing, or so terrible, that regular comparisons just won't do. Hyperbole is used when a poet wants to make a strong point about something. It is almost always funny, so be sure not to use hyperbole when you are trying to write a serious poem!

Words to Know

consistent: to stay the same.

contribute: to add to something.

torrent: a rushing stream of water.

galleon: a sailing ship used before the eighteenth century.

moor: a piece of open land.

TONE

One literary technique that is very important in any writing you do is tone. Tone is the mood of the poem. This sounds easy, but poets take a lot of time to make sure the tone is **consistent** all the way through. They want every single word to **contribute** to the tone. Otherwise the reader might be confused about what emotions the poem is trying to convey.

POEM!

The Highwayman by Alfred Noyes

The wind was a **torrent** of darkness among
  the gusty trees.

The moon was a ghostly **galleon**
  tossed upon cloudy seas.

The road was a ribbon of moonlight
  over the purple **moor**,

And the highwayman came riding—

Riding—riding—

The highwayman came riding,
  up to the old inn-door.

This is just the first six lines of a very long poem, but already you can feel the mood. What do you think the tone of this poem is? Scary? Spooky? Adventurous? How do you know?

A few phrases help us understand the tone of this poem—*torrent of darkness*, *ghostly galleon* and *ribbon of moonlight over the purple moor*. If Alfred Noyes had written, "The wind was a rainbow of light among the breezy trees," the tone would be very different. This is why it's important that every word in a poem match with the tone.

The *Highwayman* has been used in songs, novels, and movies since it was published in 1906.

Did you Know?

Tone is part of any piece of writing. When you write an email to a friend, do you want to use an angry tone? You might if you'd had a fight, but usually we use a friendly tone. What tone would you use in an essay for your teacher? A letter to your parents convincing them to let you have a later bedtime? Whether you're writing poetry, letters, or **persuasive** arguments, tone is a very important part of your work.

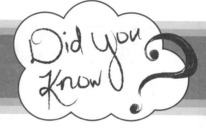

Words to Know

persuasive: able to get someone to do something.

TRY THIS! HUNT FOR LITERARY TECHNIQUES

An alliteration is the repetition of a sound at the beginning of two or more neighboring words, such as *zany zebras* or *babbling brook*. Can you find alliteration in *The Highwayman*? How about a metaphor?

METAPHOR MADNESS MATCHING

SUPPLIES
ℓ pencil
ℓ Poetry Journal

A metaphor is used to describe something by saying it is something else. They help you look at something in a different way. Mixing metaphors, though, is confusing and just doesn't sound right.

1 Look through the chart below and match the first part of the line (column one) to the second part of the line (column two) to keep the metaphors from mixing!

Column One	Column Two
The dragonfly unfolded his delicate glass wings . . .	and gasped for the slightest hint of oxygen.
The cake rose up on its hind legs . . .	and grew its own mushrooms in the produce section.
I took 12 steps into the airless dark of the tunnel . . .	and made a sound of tiny, clear bells.
The angry toddler blew smoke from its ears . . .	and shook all its frosting off its body.
The dimly lit grocery store was sticky with damp basement smell . . .	and pawed the ground with anxious fury.

2 Write out each correct sentence in your Poetry Journal.

THINK MORE: Mismatch your metaphors on purpose. Do they sound right? Can you find any second parts that fit with more than one first part? Can you think of some of your own mismatched metaphors and then make them right?

SIMILES TO SMILE ABOUT

Similes are fun to write and they make a lot of sense to read. You can create similes out of phrases you never suspected could be connected!

1 Think of seven phrases to form the first parts of your similes. Their structure will be like this: "Your breakfast was as cold as a . . ." or "The dog was as silly as a . . ." Write down your phrases and cut them out so you have seven pieces of paper. Put them in a hat.

2 Think of the last parts of your seven similes. These will sound like "stone in the snow" or "clown with the hiccups." Write these down, cut them out, and put the pieces of paper in a different hat.

3 Choose one piece of paper from the first hat. Choose one piece of paper from the second hat. Pair up your phrases and choose the next set. Keep choosing until you have chosen all of the phrases.

4 Write down the results in your Poetry Journal. Did any of your similes make sense? Are any of them creative enough to use in a poem?

The word *simile* comes from the Latin word *similis*, which means similar.

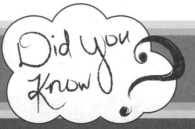

Did you know?

SUPPLIES

ℓ pencil
ℓ markers
ℓ scrap paper
ℓ Poetry Journal

HYPERBOLES ARE THE BEST LITERARY TECHNIQUE EVER!

When we're excited, we tend to use hyperbole in conversation. It's a way of expressing how we feel, and a way to get other people excited too. But hyperbole can also sound pretty silly when we look closely at our words. One way to take a closer look is to draw what we're saying.

THIS BOOK WEIGHS A TON!

1 Some examples of hyperbole are, "My sandwich is as giant as a house!" and "I'm hungry enough to eat a horse!" and "I'm so tired I could sleep forever!" Think of your own example of hyperbole.

2 Draw a picture of yourself doing your hyperbole. Be creative. Take up the whole page with your drawing.

3 A word bubble is a circled space above a person where his or her words can be written. Write your hyperbole somewhere above your drawing, circle it, and add a line connecting the word bubble to your character. Keep your drawing in your Poetry Journal.

THINK MORE: When you use hyperbole in your poems and other writing, your readers might not take you seriously. Sometimes that's just fine, but other times it's important that your readers carefully consider your words. Can you think of times when it's better not to use hyperbole in your writing?

SUPPLIES

ℓ paper
ℓ 3 or 4 friends
ℓ pen or pencil
   for each friend
ℓ hat or bowl
ℓ timer

SAY WHAT?

Tone is a very important part of reading and writing poetry. It's also a big part of spoken communication. Have fun with a group of friends in a game of Tone Charades!

1 Cut or rip the piece of paper into 10 different pieces and hand out two to three pieces to each person.

2 On each piece of paper, have everyone write a word that conveys a tone. Some examples are *happy*, *angry*, *wistful*, and *excited*. What other tone words can you think of?

3 Fold each piece of paper and put them all in the hat or bowl.

4 The first player picks a piece of paper and looks at the tone word without letting the other players see. The player has 30 seconds to act out that word without speaking. It's easier if you act out a scene in which you might be feeling that word. For example, if you get the word *excited*, you pretend someone just gave you a present and you're jumping up and down with a happy look on your face.

5 The other players try to guess which tone word the player is trying to convey. Whoever guesses first is the next player to pick a word! Play until all the words have been used.

FIND ANOTHER FOUND POEM

Here's another way to find a found poem. Once you have the knack for discovering poems, you'll find poetry everywhere!

SUPPLIES

- ℓ magazine, newspaper, or book that nobody else wants to read
- ℓ pencil
- ℓ scissors
- ℓ piece of cardboard
- ℓ glue

1 Read a couple of articles or pages of a magazine, book, or newspaper. Try to find something you're interested in so your poem will have more meaning for you.

2 Lightly circle words that contribute to the meaning of the article. For example, if the article is about wild animals, circle the words that describe how the wild animals look and behave. If your article is about schools, circle words that refer to students, teachers, classrooms, and backpacks. Circle lightly so you can erase later on.

3 Cut out the words you circled. Trim any extra words around your word if you need to.

4 Arrange your words on the piece of cardboard. Don't worry about keeping them in the same order as they appeared in the article! Spend some time rearranging them until you find an order that you like. Try reading your words out loud to see how they sound next to each other. Can you use any literary techniques in your found poem? Which ones?

5 Once you find a poem you like, glue the words down. Don't forget a title! Put your found poem in your Poetry Journal.

THINK ABOUT IT: A few poets who write found poetry have been accused of plagiarism, which is when someone copies someone else. When a poet makes a poem out of words he or she finds in a news article, do you think that's plagiarism? Why or why not?

Words to Know

somber: very sad and serious.

cadence: the way a person's voice rises and falls while he or she is speaking.

KNOW YOUR POETS: DYLAN THOMAS

Born in Wales, which is a part of the United Kingdom, Dylan Thomas (1914–1953) worked as a newspaper reporter before becoming a poet. He had a very specific style when he read his poems out loud. Here he reads a very **somber** poem about death. How does this poem make you feel when you hear it? How does his voice contribute to the poem's solemn tone? What about the **cadence** of his words? How is this poem different from the poem you listened to on page 21? How are they similar?

DYLAN THOMAS

 PS **Listen to Dylan Thomas read.**

THE SOUNDS WE HEAR

Since poetry existed before writing was invented, the way a poem sounds has always been very important. Most poets still expect that their poetry will be heard with ears in addition to being read with eyes.

Because of this, poets focus on both what their words mean and what their words sound like. You've learned about some of the literary techniques that help emphasize a poem's meaning. There are also techniques that emphasize what a poem sounds like when it's read out loud.

LINE BREAKS AND STANZAS

You've learned that shape poems make certain shapes on the page. But what about other forms of poems? What shape does an epic poem or a haiku make?

Their shapes may not have a name, but the way the words are grouped together affect the way we read and hear the poem. A **line break** is one way that a poet lets us know how to read the poem. A line break happens when the poet moves the words from one line to another.

POEM!

Boom, Boom, Ain't It Great To Be Crazy?
A horse and a flea and three blind mice
Sat on a tombstone shooting dice.
The horse slipped and fell on the flea—
"Whoops!" said the flea. "There's a horse on me!"

The line breaks in this poem happen at the words *mice*, *dice*, *flea*, and *me*.

When you read a poem out loud, you usually **pause** at the end of a line of poetry. Often there is a **punctuation mark**, such as a period, comma, colon, or semicolon, but not always! Even if there's no punctuation mark, it's still a good idea to pause your voice at the end of a line break.

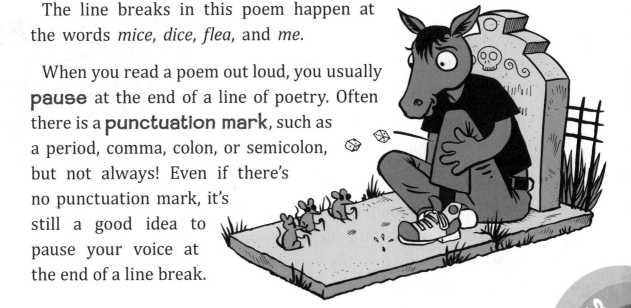

Words to Know

line break: the point at which two lines of text are split.

pause: a brief stop or rest.

punctuation mark: a **symbol** such as a period or a question mark that is used to make writing clear and understandable.

symbol: an image that stands for something else.

BOOM BOOM!

Poetry can be sung out loud! Listen to a song version of *Boom, Boom, Ain't It Great To Be Crazy?* How does the music add to the rhythm of the words? Is it easier to remember as a song?

Stanzas are groups of lines that go together. There are three common types of stanzas:

* couplets have two lines that usually rhyme

* tercets have three lines that might or might not rhyme

* quatrains have four lines that might or might not rhyme

American poet Emily Dickinson often wrote in quatrains.

Hope is the thing with feathers
That perches in the soul,
And sings the tune without the words,
And never stops at all . . .

POEM!

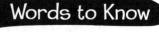
Words to Know

stanza: a group of lines that form a part of a poem.

Why did the poet go to the hospital?

JUST **4** FUN

Because he couldn't stanza!

Some poets put more or fewer lines in their stanzas, depending on what they feel the poem needs. Stanzas are useful for grouping ideas together in a poem. They are also good for breaking up the sounds and keeping rhymes together to make them more effective.

PUNCTUATION

Punctuation is important in any kind of writing, even poetry. This chart will help you remember what marks to use—and where to use them—in your poetry, stories, essays, and letters.

What it looks like	What it's called	What it means	Example
.	period	ends a sentence	The fox and bear are friends.
?	question mark	ends a question	Are the fox and giraffe friends?
,	comma	pauses a sentence	The fox, bear, and giraffe are going to have a party.
!	exclamation point	ends a sentence with excitement	The fox and bear are excited!
;	semicolon	joins two separate sentences about the same subject	The fox is excited; the giraffe is calm.
—	em dash	adds a longer pause	The fox is happy— it's his birthday!
:	colon	starts a list	The fox thinks of friends to invite: the porcupine, the mole, and the chicken.

In the 1400s, periods were used to mark both the end of a sentence and a pause—even in the middle of a sentence! It took about 60 years before periods were used only to end sentences, and commas and semicolons became the marks for pauses.

Did you know?

ALLITERATION

Alliteration happens when the poet uses words together that have the same sounds or that start with the same letter.

POEM!

The Raven by Edgar Allan Poe

Once upon a midnight dreary, while I
  pondered, weak and weary,

Over many a quaint and curious volume of forgotten lore—

While I nodded, nearly napping, suddenly
  there came a tapping,

As of some one gently rapping, rapping at my chamber door.

"'Tis some visitor," I muttered, "tapping at my
  chamber door—

Only this and nothing more."

This famous poem uses several examples of alliteration: *weak and weary*, *quaint and curious*, *nodded nearly napping*, and *rapping rapping*. The way these words sound alike, rhyme, and reflect each other make the poem very easy and fun to read out loud. They also make it easier to memorize the poem.

Alliteration makes a poem sound interesting to a reader's or listener's ears. Human brains like it when words that sound alike are paired together and spoken out loud. That's why you can find lots of alliteration in advertising or in the names of stores, such as Dunkin' Donuts, Best Buy, and Chuck E. Cheese.

Another form of writing that's based on alliteration is a tongue twister.

How much wood
Would a woodchuck chuck
If a woodchuck
Could chuck
Wood?

David's father has three sons. Their names are Snap, Crackle, and . . . ?

JUST **4** FUN

David!

This tongue twister uses lots of alliteration to make it hard for people to speak the words quickly. How many words can you find that start with *w*? How many words rhyme? How many start with or have the *ch* sound? What happens when you try to say these words very quickly?

Sometimes alliteration makes a line easier to say, and sometimes alliteration makes a line harder to say!

Did you Know?

ONOMATOPOEIA

Thunk. Boink. Meow. Each of these words is an example of **onomatopoeia**. Pronounce it like this: ON-oh-MA-toh-PEE-ya. An onomatopoeia is a word that sounds just like the sound it's describing. Say the word *meow* out loud. Now try *hiss*. Now try *desk*. Does *desk* sound like a desk? Some people might think so, but in general, desk is not considered to be an onomatopoeia because the word *desk* doesn't sound like an actual desk.

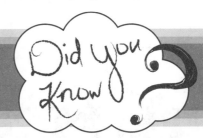

Words to Know

onomatopoeia: a word that sounds like its meaning.

BOINK!

Think of a rubber ball bouncing off your forehead. *Boink* is a word someone watching you might say out loud. *Boink* might be very similar to the sound you heard when the ball made contact with your head!

An onomatopoeia is a fun word to use in poetry. It makes readers experience the poem beyond simply reading the words on the page, even if the reader doesn't realize it. When a word such as *meow* appears in a poem, you may not consciously think of a cat, but your brain automatically gives you the picture of a cat.

KNOW YOUR POETS: SHEL SILVERSTEIN

Shel Silverstein was born in 1930 and first wrote cartoons and songs for adults. Eventually he discovered his audience of children, and became famous for lots of poems and picture books. Perhaps his most famous book is a poem called *The Giving Tree*, which is about a tree that gives up her apples, branches, and trunk for the little boy she loves.

EDGE

SHEL SILVERSTEIN

PS Read Shel Silverstein's poems and watch short animations based on his work.

TRY THIS! WATER ONOMATOPOEIA

Sometimes lots of different words can describe the sound of one thing using onomatopoeia. How many words can you think of that describe the action of water? Here are a couple to start you off: glug, gush, flow.

This works for words you don't know as well, too. What about this phrase from a poem by Alfred Lord Tennyson: "And the murmuring of innumerable bees." What does it make you think of? Even if you don't know what murmuring is, or what it means to be innumerable, you might still get a sense of what Alfred Lord Tennyson is writing about. Still curious? Look in the glossary for these definitions.

An onomatopoeia can be different in each language, even when it's describing the same sound. For example, the sound of a clock is "tick tock" in English and "katchin katchin" in Japanese.

Did you Know?

ASSONANCE AND CONSONANCE

You've learned about rhyming words, but did you know that sounds within words can make rhymes, too? When these sounds are vowel sounds (a, e, i, o, u, and sometimes y), the rhyme is called **assonance**. When the sounds are from consonants (all the other letters), the rhyme is called **consonance**.

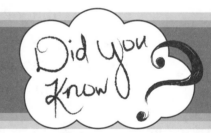

Words to Know

assonance: the repetition of a vowel sound.

consonance: the repetition of a consonant sound.

49

This poem contains examples of assonance and consonance. Examples of assonance are underlined and examples of consonance are in bold.

POEM!

Fire and Ice by Robert Frost

Some **s**<u>ay</u> the world
  will end in f<u>i</u>re,

Some **s**<u>ay</u> in <u>i</u>ce.

From what <u>I</u>'ve
  t<u>a</u>sted of de<u>s</u>ire

<u>I</u> hold with those who f<u>a</u>vor fire.

But if it had to perish tw<u>i</u>ce,

<u>I</u> think <u>I</u> know enough of h<u>a</u>te

To **s**<u>ay</u> that for destruction <u>i</u>ce

Is al**s**o gr<u>ea</u>t

And would suff<u>i</u>ce.

The *s* and *ay* sounds keep repeating. What other sounds repeat? How do these repeating sounds contribute to the way you hear the poem? When you read the poem out loud, do these sounds make it easier or harder to say?

Robert Frost asked an astronomer named Harlow Shapley, "How is the world going to end?" Shapley answered it would either be burnt by the sun or plunged into a permanent ice age. Frost was inspired to write this poem.

When you write poetry, you have to think about what the words mean. But you also have to think about what the words sound like when strung together. Finding the balance between meaning and sound is a large part of a poet's job.

ONOMATOPOEIA FOR DINNER

SUPPLIES

- ℓ paper
- ℓ pencil
- ℓ markers
- ℓ Poetry Journal

Once you learn about onomatopoeia, these words start showing up everywhere! One place these words really like to hang out is the dinner table. Especially when there is fried chicken! Throw an imaginary dinner party for some of the noisiest people you can think of.

1 Make your menu! What food offers lots of opportunity for words that are onomatopoeia? Remember, these words sound like the things they're describing. Write a list of foods that are noisy to eat in your Poetry Journal.

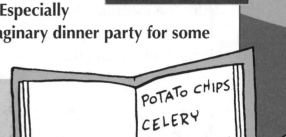

POTATO CHIPS
CELERY
CORN FLAKES
BUBBLE GU

2 Who are you going to invite for dinner? Some people are more likely to make noise while they eat than others! Consider inviting babies, dogs, people with no teeth, people who talk while they eat, and people who like to burp. At this dinner table, manners are less important than onomatopoeia.

3 Now draw your collection of noisy eaters at your dinner table! Don't forget to put food on their plates. Above your figures, write the onomatopoeia that goes with each person in a word bubble. A person with no teeth might be saying "Glump, glump, glump." The baby might be saying "Yam, yam, yam." Keep your drawing in your Poetry Journal.

SUPPLIES

ℓ 3 or 4 friends

RHYME TIME

Rhyming is one of the hardest things to do in a poem. Sometimes, the poet concentrates so hard on the rhyme that he or she forgets to make sure the meaning, tone, and sound of the words are right. Rhyming can be fun, too. It's especially fun to work with rhyming words out loud instead of writing them down. You can do this activity in a group or on your own. This can be a fun game to play on a long car ride.

1 Choose a familiar fairy tale, such as *The Three Little Pigs*. Say the first line of the fairy tale as well as you can remember it.

Once upon a time, three little pigs left home to find their way in the world.

2 The next person says the next line and makes it rhyme with the first line. Then he or she adds a new line that doesn't rhyme.

The first little pig, his tail was curled.
He walked for a while, then found some sticks.

3 The next person says the next line and makes a rhyme with the one before, and then adds a new line.

He built his house in tall grass and worried about ticks.
But the big bad wolf came along and scared him even more.

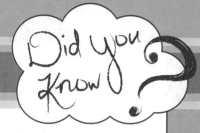

4 Keep going until everyone has had a chance to make a rhyme. Don't be worried about following the original fairy tale, or even about trying to get your rhyming poem to make sense. This is a fun exercise for your brain to practice rhyming!

KNOW YOUR POETS: GERTRUDE STEIN

Gertrude Stein (1874–1946) was born in the United States but moved to France when she was 29 years old. She was known for being good friends with many different artists and writers of that time period, and had a large collection of art. Most of what she wrote was for adults, but some of her poetry is great for kids! Read Gertrude Stein's poem *A Very Valentine* to yourself, and then listen to Gertrude Stein read it aloud. Does the poem sound different when she reads it? In what ways?

A Very Valentine

Very fine is my valentine.

Very fine and very mine.

Very mine is my valentine very mine and very fine.

Very fine is my valentine and mine, very fine
    very mine and mine is my valentine.

POEM!

  Listen to Gertrude Stein reading *A Very Valentine*.

GERTRUDE STEIN

53

SUPPLIES

ℓ pencil
ℓ Poetry Journal

SNOWMAN STANZA

Using stanzas is a useful way to organize your poems. Write a poem about winter with a snowman stanza!

1 Trace or copy the snowman template on the next page onto a blank page in your Poetry Journal.

2 Draw a snowman's face on the top snowball so he can watch you write his poem.

3 In the middle snowball, write five lines of poetry that start with these phrases. The lines are fill-in-the-blank.

Winter is _____ and _____.

I like to _____ and _____.

I feel _____ and _____.

I smell _____ and _____.

Winter is _____ and _____.

4 In the bottom snowball, write five lines of poetry about the snowman. You can use the same lines and replace *I* with *Snowman*, or you can make up your own. Be sure to keep in mind that you are writing about wintery things, so your images should be cold ones!

TRY MORE! Make up your own poem about another season, choosing a different drawing and different phrases.

SNOWMAN TEMPLATE:
TRACE OR COPY THIS INTO YOUR POETRY JOURNAL

SUPPLIES

ℓ pencil
ℓ paper
ℓ Poetry Journal

A COUPLE OF RHYMING COUPLETS

You can write a rhyming poem by stringing together a series of rhyming couplets. A couplet is two lines of poetry. It's easier to start with two rhyming words than several rhyming words! Here's an example of a poem made from couplets.

Lunch Bunch

The bear woke up and wanted berries for lunch,

So he headed to the woods because he had a hunch

There'd be blueberries there, and strawberries, too.

And if any people came 'round he'd scare them away, "Shoo!"

A little girl walked up as he was sitting down to eat

And calmly spread her own lunch on a sheet

And asked the bear, "Would you like to share?"

The bear was frightened and bolted out of there!

1 Think of something to write about. You may have an idea, or you can choose one from your idea rocks bag from page 24.

2 Write a list of things about your topic. These can be descriptions of characters, events, actions, or the setting. Choose the item on your list that you find the most interesting and create your first line. Don't make this line a complete sentence— instead, make it the introductory phrase, the first part of what you want to say.

WOULD YOU LIKE TO SHARE?

3 For your next line, finish the thought you started in the first line. Make it rhyme. You might need to write down lots of words that rhyme with the last word of your first line before you find one that works.

4 Write as many couplets as you need to tell the story of your poem. You'll want to make revisions to your poem until you feel it's just right. Then copy your final draft in your Poetry Journal. Don't forget a title!

KNOW YOUR POETS: EDNA ST. VINCENT MILLAY

Edna St. Vincent Millay (1892–1950) was an American poet who also wrote plays. She was the third woman to ever win the Pulitzer Prize for Poetry, one of the highest poetry honors. She often wrote poems in iambic pentameter. Lines of iambic pentameter contain 10 syllables, or five pairs of syllables, in a certain rhythm. Say the words, "I am" out loud five times. You're speaking in iambic pentameter! The first syllable is not stressed and the second syllable is stressed, so it sounds like this: da **DUM** da **DUM** da **DUM** da **DUM** da **DUM**. Listen for iambic pentameter in these lines by Millay.

I know I am but summer to your heart,
And not the full four seasons of the year;
And you must welcome from another part
Such noble moods as are not mine, my dear.

EDNA ST. VINCENT MILLAY

POEM!

57

SUPPLIES

ℓ pencil
ℓ Poetry Journal

A GLASS OF WATER IS A DROP OF RELIEF

Remember, an onomatopoeia is a word that sounds like its meaning. A metaphor describes something by saying it is something else. A simile compares one thing to another using the words *like* or *as*. And hyperbole is an exaggerated description of something.

1 What does each of the following activities look, sound, taste, hear, or feel like? Give your answers as an onomatopoeia, metaphor, simile, or hyperbole. Write your answers in your Poetry Journal.

Activity	Your Answer
A train wreck . . .	is a box of Legos thrown down the stairs.
A day at the beach . . .	tastes like a sandy coconut popsicle.
A fight at the playground . . .	
Getting an A on a test you studied hard for . . .	
Losing the championship game . . .	
Forgetting to take out the trash and getting in trouble . . .	
Arguing with your brother or sister . . .	
When your best friend moves away . . .	
Winning the school spelling bee . . .	

POETRY, MUSIC, AND MATH

What does poetry have to do with music or math? How often do you hear poems read on the radio? Do math teachers ever speak in verse? Writing, music, and math are all made up of patterns. Just as poets use word patterns to create poems, musicians use musical patterns to create songs, and mathematicians use number patterns to create equations.

In a poem, if the word pattern isn't right, the poem doesn't sound right. In music, if the pattern of notes is off, the music sounds terrible. In math, if the number pattern is wrong, the equation doesn't add up.

Words to Know

verse: a part of a poem or song.

equation: a sentence using mathematical symbols that states two things are the same.

Words to Know

expertise: special skills or knowledge.

critically: carefully thinking about what is good or bad about something, or what is right or wrong about it.

lyricist: someone who writes the words to a song.

lyrics: the words of a song.

melancholy: sadness.

The patterns that form our experience of music, math, and poetry are similar. If we learn to understand one, than we'll have an easier time learning to understand the others.

This doesn't mean that by becoming a poet you'll automatically know how to do math! **Expertise** comes from practice. But it does mean that learning to read and think **critically** about poems will make it easier to think critically about other subjects. You'll have stronger brain muscles!

MUSIC

Song **lyricists** use rhymes, rhythm, alliteration, metaphor, and simile to write their songs. These are all literary techniques that poets use! The difference between song **lyrics** and poems is that songs are set to music. The music adds another layer of sound and meaning that poems don't have.

The music has a lot of influence over the tone of the song. Even when the lyrics are happy ones, if the music itself is **melancholy**, then the whole thing will feel sad. Can you think of a song that has sad or scary lyrics and happy music? Does the song make you feel happy or sad?

Why do hummingbirds hum?

JUST **4** FUN

They forgot the words!

Even music without words has connections to poetry. Patterns appear in these **compositions** as well. When you listen to a song without words, how does it make you feel different things? How does it create tone? When you hum, can you make your humming sad or happy? What changes?

Words to Know

composition: a piece of music.

major note: a musical note in the major scale that can sound upbeat.

minor note: a musical note in the minor scale that can sound sad.

HMMM
MM HMM
MMM!

BOO HOO HOO!

Music has two different kinds of notes, **major notes** and **minor notes**. Major notes tend to sound happier, and minor notes tend to sound sadder.

OLD POEMS, NEW MUSIC

American folk singer Natalie Merchant has made an album of songs based on children's poetry from the 1800s. Listen to one of these songs and read the lyrics as they appear on the screen. Does the music match the poetry? Do the words have the same impact on today's audience as they might have had on children from the 1800s?

Words can sound happy or sad, too. Read the following lists of words and decide whether they are happy words or sad words.

English	French
sunshine	jolie
thunderstorm	fleur
breakfast	escalier
farewell	jardin
bleak	grimper
sugar	velo
snapping	jaune
umbrella	mal

Words to Know

evoke: to bring a picture or feelings to someone's mind.

political oppression: when a group, such as the government, treats citizens unfairly.

For some words, the meaning will dictate the tone. But what about words you don't know the meaning of, such as those on the French list?

You might still get a sense of their tones. The way something sounds can affect what emotion it **evokes** in the reader or listener. The different vibrations that different sounds create affect our brains in different ways. This is why major musical notes generally sound happier than minor musical notes.

Many poets use poetry to talk about equal rights or protest events such as war and political oppression.

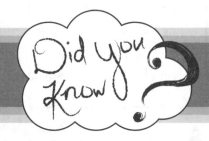

KNOW YOUR POETS: LANGSTON HUGHES

Before Langston Hughes (1902–1967) was 12 years old, he had lived in six different cities! He also visited lots of different countries during his life and held many different jobs. He was African American and wrote poems that told stories about the lives of African Americans. He was also an activist who worked for equal rights for people. Langston Hughes's poems are sometimes called jazz poems, because they reflect the smooth tone and easy rhythm of jazz music, which became popular in the 1920s.

LANGSTON HUGHES

You can read one of his poems here.

Songs that are played at a faster pace often sound happier, angrier, more excited, or more enthusiastic than songs that are played at a slower pace. Some musicians will deliberately slow a song down to change its tone. This is just like a poet adding more line breaks to slow down a poem.

MATH MATTERS

It makes sense that poetry and music have a lot in common, but what about poetry and math? How is math anything like poetry?

Just as with poetry and music, math is made up of patterns.

* ✳ 2 + 2 = 4
* ✳ 2 + 3 = 5
* ✳ 2 + 4 = 6
* ✳ 2 + 5 = 7

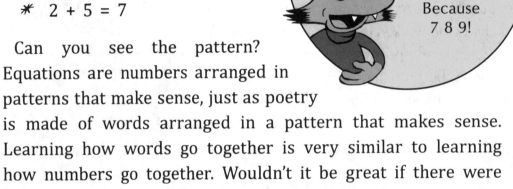

Why was 6 afraid of 7?

JUST **4** FUN

Because 7 8 9!

Can you see the pattern? Equations are numbers arranged in patterns that make sense, just as poetry is made of words arranged in a pattern that makes sense. Learning how words go together is very similar to learning how numbers go together. Wouldn't it be great if there were a calculator for words?

Some poets use the structure of equations to create poems. These could be considered shape poems. The words are arranged in a very specific way. Symbols from math are used as part of the poems, such as in this one.

POEM!

Four Squared Meals

2 kids + 2 bowls of cereal = ready for a day at camp!

2 kids + 3 peanut butter sandwiches = lunchtime recharge!

2 kids + 4 carrot sticks = healthy snack mom makes us eat!

2 kids + 5 slices of pizza = full bellies for late night giggles!

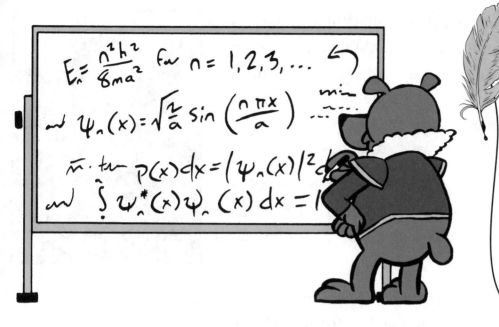

Words to Know

rigid: a certain way, not easily changed or unable to bend.

strict: following the rules exactly.

analytical: breaking down problems into small parts to find solutions.

When you write a poem using math symbols, it can be a lot of fun to discover how creative you can be within a **rigid** structure. Remember writing haiku and having to use just 17 syllables? Did that force you to try new ways of arranging words? Many poets love working within **strict** guidelines because it makes them discover new ways of expressing their thoughts.

Albert Einstein, perhaps the most famous mathematician in history, also loved music. He played his violin or piano when he got stuck on a problem.

Advanced math requires **analytical** and creative thinking. Many mathematicians listen to music, look at art, or read poetry when they're working hard at solving problems. By immersing yourself in art, you sometimes find the answers you've been looking for.

There is beauty in art as well. While something one person finds beautiful might not have any attraction for someone else, there are examples of beauty that almost everyone agrees upon. *The Mona Lis*a. Sunsets. Music by Mozart. Babies. The view of Earth from space. And poetry.

When poetry is written well, it's beautiful. It sounds right, and it feels right. It doesn't matter if the poem is happy or sad, a well-written poem is a beautiful thing.

Math is the same way. People who understand math will often refer to certain equations as beautiful. They look right. They feel right. They compute the right numbers.

Think creatively about what makes something beautiful. Whether it's poetry, math, songs, or science, we can learn how to develop that beauty in whatever it is we're creating.

FRACTALS IN NATURE

Fractals are a great example of patterns in math. There's a way to explain fractals using advanced mathematical terms and concepts, but there's also another way. Fractals are made of repeating patterns that you can see up close or from farther away. This means that if you look at a fractal close up it will be made of the same repeating shapes as when you look at it from a distance. Think of a fern or a Queen Ann's lace flower. If you look closely at the blossom, you'll find the same shapes repeating over and over on a smaller and smaller scale.

POEM!

POETRY EQUATIONS

You've learned that poets often find structure inspiring. What's more structured than a mathematical formula?

Here's an example of an equation poem using A + B = C.

Winter Kitchen

snow day + mom stays home = beef stew dinner

 +  =

1 Choose a mathematical formula to use for your equation poem. You might want to start with a simple one, such as A + B = C.

2 Decide on the topic of your poem and start brainstorming. Make a list of all the things you can think of that have anything to do with your topic.

3 Replace the letters in your equation with words. Rearrange your words until they sound good and mean something. It might take a few tries. You may discover you need to use a different equation. That's fine—it's all part of the creative process!

4 Copy your poem in your Poetry Journal and decorate it.

SHAKE YOUR MUSIC MAKER

Even songs with no words are very similar to poetry. Patterns in music are like patterns in poems. See if you can find the patterns in the music you and your friends create.

1 Everyone choose a noisemaker. If you don't have one, you can tap on the table with a pencil, drum on your knees, clap your hands, or make a noise with your mouth.

2 Start making a sound with your noisemaker. Think about the beat you want to create. You might add some rhythm, too. Make that noise for several seconds on your own.

3 Another person starts making a different sound with his or her noisemaker. The beat should be similar, but maybe the second person will use a different rhythm to add a new layer of sound to the music.

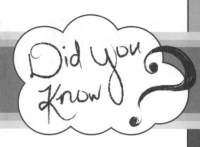

4 Add a third person, and a fourth person. It might be hard to keep your own rhythm! Often a bunch of people making noise will eventually fall into the same beat and rhythm—try to stay focused on keeping your sound going. What is the tone of your music? Can you hear patterns?

THINK ABOUT IT: What did the music sound like with everyone using a different rhythm? Did the rhythms match up in surprising ways? Do you think this is how an orchestra plays together? How is the music you were making like a poem?

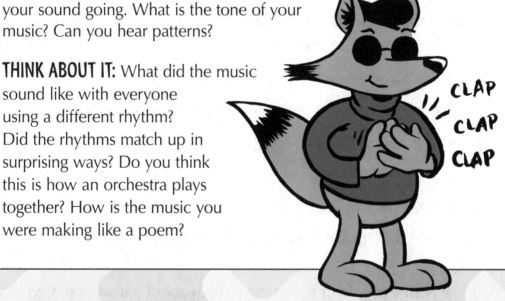

CLAP

CLAP

CLAP

WATER MUSIC

Listen to George Frideric Handel's *Water Music*. Can you pick out repeating patterns? Are there parts of the music that seem to go together like lines in a stanza of poetry? Is this music major or minor?

PS Try listening to more pieces of classical music and pick up the patterns in the notes that give the music its character.

A RECTANGLE IS A WINDOW IS A DOOR

Geometry is the study of shapes—squares, circles, triangles, spheres, cones. They all have certain properties that make them that shape, just as poems have different properties that make them limericks, haiku, and epics! In this activity you'll combine math and poetry to write a diamante poem.

SUPPLIES

- paper
- pencil
- markers, crayons, or other decorating supplies
- Poetry Journal

A diamante poem has seven lines. It's written with this structure:

1 One word that is the name of the shape

2 Two adjectives that describe the shape

3 Three verbs ending in "-ing" that describe the shape

4 Four nouns related to the shape

5 Three verbs ending in "-ing" that describe the shape

6 Two adjectives that describe the shape

7 One word that is the name of the shape

Here is an example of a diamante poem about a diamond. Can you see the pattern?

Diamond
Pointy, four-sided
Sparkling, digging, wishing
Ring, star, window, clown eyes
Winking, spinning, waiting
Transparent, sharp
Diamond

1 Think of a shape. You might choose a circle, square, diamond, or something else. What properties does that shape have? Are there edges? Are there angles? How many? Write down all the ways you can describe your shape. These are the properties of your shape.

2 Now think about your shape in the real world. What is it used for? Do you usually find your shape alone or with other shapes like it? Is your shape rare or do you see it frequently? Do you see your shape in nature, in cities, in the air, or on the ground? Ask your friends and family if they have any ideas about your shape. Make a list of things you know about your shape.

3 Now you try it! Write a diamante poem about your shape, using your lists of properties and ideas. Be creative.

4 Revise your poem. Are all of your words the best words for your poem? Does your poem make you think about something else beside your shape? Is the first letter of each line capitalized? Always check your spelling! Copy your diamante poem into your Poetry Journal and decorate it.

SEASONAL POETRY MOBILE

Many poets are inspired by the seasons! You can find lots of poems about winter, spring, summer, and fall by looking in a poetry anthology. Seasonal poems are fun to read out loud or to yourself, and they also make great art.

1 Which season is your favorite? Choose a poem with that season as its subject and print it out. With an adult's permission, you can find poems on the Internet or at your library.

2 Draw seasonal shapes on the heavy paper. If your season is winter, you might draw the outline of a snowflake or a snowman. Draw at least four shapes and cut them out.

3 Cut your poem into as many pieces as you have shapes. If you have four shapes, cut four pieces. Make sure you cut your poem so you can still read all the words!

4 Glue your pieces of poem to your shapes and decorate both sides of your shapes.

5 Punch a hole in the top of each shape. Cut your string into as many different pieces as you have shapes, and make sure they are all different lengths. Tie one end of each string to a shape and the other end to the coat hanger. Hang your mobile where every shape can swing freely!

SUPPLIES

- ℓ printed lines from a seasonal poem
- ℓ pencil
- ℓ cardboard or heavy paper
- ℓ scissors
- ℓ glue
- ℓ markers
- ℓ glitter glue, stickers, paint, crayons
- ℓ hole puncher
- ℓ string or yarn
- ℓ coat hanger

When you read a poem, what happens to you? Do poems make you tired, happy, sad, or energized? Do you ever feel like you get shivers from a poem? Does it ever change your mood?

You've learned a lot so far about the **mechanics** of poetry. This is how words fit together and why they sometimes fit well and sometimes they clash. But why do we write and read poetry?

Words to Know

mechanics: the working parts of something.

It's not like food. We won't die if we never read poetry. It's not even like playing a video game, where you're trying to reach a goal before the zombies eat your brain. So, why poetry?

CHILLIN'

Have you ever felt chills on the back of your neck or down your spine? They seem to come out of nowhere. You might be

watching a movie, talking to your dad, or listening to music when Oh! Chills!

These chills have nothing to do with temperature. These kinds of chills happen when your brain is flooded with a chemical called dopamine. Dopamine is a natural chemical found in your body. When it triggers certain points in your brain, you feel good.

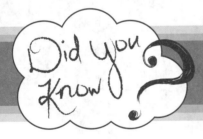

Dopamine is the chemical that helps you stay awake when you feel sleepy.

Dopamine also floods your brain when you listen to music you love, when you snuggle with a favorite person or pet, and even when you eat certain foods. It's a good sensation, isn't it?

Sometimes people try so hard to get those chills, they resort to negative behavior such as eating too much cake or taking drugs. Poetry, though, is a very healthy way of getting the chills!

Scientists aren't sure why we get chills when we read poetry or listen to music. Humans and other animals have many useful behaviors that have helped us survive, such as running away when we're scared. Can you think why an animal might **hibernate** in winter or why a bird would build its nest high in a tree? Reading poetry doesn't seem like a behavior that would help us survive.

Words to Know

hibernate: to sleep through the winter.

socialized: to do things with other people in a friendly way.

literature: written work such as poems, plays, and novels.

Some studies suggest that figuring out hard sentences and words keeps our brains working well as we get old. Scientists think that our brains' responses to poetry and music keep us **socialized** within our human group. **Literature** makes us want to be with each other. Whatever the answer is, it's nice to know that reading poetry is never a waste of time, according to your body!

THE FEELINGS WE FEEL

Many people love to read and write poetry because of the way it makes them feel. Poems can make us feel different things, just like a picture of puppies playing on the grass makes us feel differently than a picture of dark clouds right before a thunderstorm. A poem about ice cream makes us feel different emotions than a poem about a grandmother who died.

Poems are good for inspiring feelings because they use very specific words. Stories and novels are much longer than poems, and use many more words. Poets have to choose their words very carefully. They are working in a smaller space and don't have room to waste on words that aren't quite right.

Reading poetry requires people to create pictures in their heads of what they're reading. To do this, people use the same skills that scientists, mathematicians, artists, and entrepreneurs use to solve the major questions of our world.

Poets continually ask themselves, "Is this the best word for what I mean?" They try to choose words that exactly convey the emotions they want to express in their poems.

Have you ever had a really great day? Maybe it was your birthday and your mom let you eat cake for breakfast and all the kids at school sang "Happy Birthday" to you. Maybe you felt so terrific when you got home from school that you wanted to share how good you felt.

Those good feelings might inspire you to write a poem. It would feel extra good to get your feelings down in writing. Then you could read your poem several weeks later and feel that good all over again.

KNOW YOUR POETS: WILLIAM WORDSWORTH

William Wordsworth (1770–1850) was an English poet. His mother died when he was very young, and three of his five children died as well. These deaths influenced his poetry, which was very **lyrical** and written with simple words and phrases.

He wrote, "Poetry is the spontaneous overflow of powerful feelings . . . " He's saying that poetry comes from emotion. Everyone has emotions. Happy, sad, scared, and anxious are all emotions that everyone experiences. Why does emotion inspire poetry?

WILLIAM WORDSWORTH

This works with bad feelings, too. Maybe your day was rotten. You forgot your homework, it was rainy, and your best friend said she wasn't going to be your best friend anymore. You get home from school and all you want to do is punch some pillows, but instead you pick up a pen and write a poem.

Words to Know

lyrical: artistically beautiful and expressive.

FRIENDSHIP OVER!

A lot of the time, after you write a poem about how bad you feel, the bad feelings go away. If you read your poem several weeks later, you might realize how low you felt that day. What a relief not to feel that way still!

Words to Know

empathy: the ability to share the feelings of others.

What about people who read poetry? Does reading a poem help make you feel less alone? Absolutely! Reading a poem activates your brain by asking you to recognize different symbols and patterns. It also affects your gut by asking you to feel **empathy** toward the subject of the poem. Empathy happens when you feel what someone else might be feeling.

Why did the cookie always write sad poems?

JUST 4 FUN

Because he was feeling crummy!

If your friend is telling you that he is feeling anxious about a spelling test, you might start to feel anxious, too. Maybe you know your spelling words really well. But since your friend is worried, you're worried with him. This is empathy, and it's a good feeling. It expands your way of thinking about the world and the people around you.

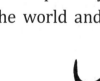

Did you Know?

Have you ever noticed yawns are contagious? When your friend yawns, you might yawn, too. Some studies have found that contagious yawning is linked to empathy, but scientists still consider yawning a mystery.

Empathy is a little different than **sympathy**. You can feel sympathy for your friend who didn't study his spelling words. This means you feel bad that he's feeling bad. But you don't share his emotion of worry. When you have empathy for someone, you actually feel the emotion he is feeling.

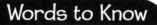

Words to Know

sympathy: the feeling that you care about someone else's problems.

Empathy works with good feelings, too! It isn't just for negative feelings such as anxiety or sadness. If you are empathetic, you can also feel good because other people feel good!

KNOW YOUR POETS: PHILLIS WHEATLEY

Phillis Wheatley (1753–1784) was born in Africa but was captured and brought to Boston as a slave. The family that bought her realized she was very smart, and decided to teach her how to read and write instead of making her work. In 1773, she published a book of poems called *Poems on Various Subjects*. This was the first book of poetry published by a slave, the first published by an African American in the United States, and the third published by a woman.

You can read one of her poems here.

PHILLIS WHEATLEY

19

BRAINY GAMES

Brains are amazing things. One amazing thing they do is try to anticipate what a word or picture is going to be. It means you might see something that isn't actually there! This is called an optical illusion.

Here's an example of an optical illusion:

Do you see a triangle? Do you see circles? Where are the lines of the triangle? Are there really lines, or is your brain just sticking them in because of the way the circles make the shapes of angles?

1 Now make your own optical illusion. Lightly trace the outline of your hand, and a little bit of your wrist.

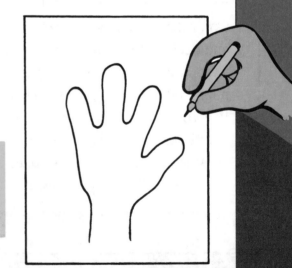

2 With your black marker, starting from the bottom of the page, draw a line all the way across the page. Make an upward curve where the line crosses your wrist. Repeat this all the way up the page with lines about a quarter of an inch apart. Whenever your line crosses your hand or fingers, make it curve up.

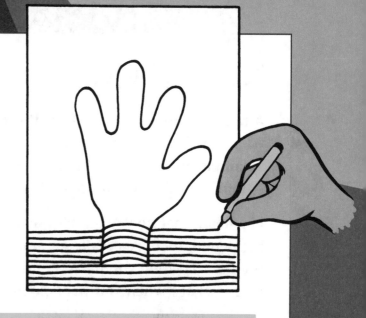

3 Use your markers to color between the lines, following the curve of the black line. What do you see when you're done? What is your hand doing? Why does it look like that?

KNOW YOUR POETS: ANNA AKHMATOVA

Anna Akhmatova (1889–1966) lived in Russia. At the time, the government treated many of its citizens badly by arresting and even killing people who spoke out against it. Akhmatova felt that it was her job to stay and write poems about what was happening in Russia, even as many of her friends were moving to other countries. Many of her poems are about the hardships faced by the Russian people.

You can read one of her poems here.

ANNA AKHMATOVA

SUPPLIES
ℓ pencil
ℓ paper
ℓ Poetry Journal

POETRY EMOTION

A famous poet named William Wordsworth, who lived in the 1700s, defined poetry as "the spontaneous overflow of powerful feelings: it takes its origin from emotion recollected in tranquility."

He meant that poetry bubbles up after something eventful has happened, such as a really great party or a bad grade or a happy day at the beach. When you think about the emotions you had during these events, that's when you write poetry.

1 Can you think about an event in your life that had a lot of emotion connected to it? It could be something that happened to you when you were much younger or just last week. It could be a sad, happy, or embarrassing event. If you can still feel those feelings even now that it's over, you'll know it's a good pick.

2 Make a list of the emotions you felt during the event. Include everything, even if some of them are the opposite of others. Maybe the day started out happy and then turned sad, or started out sad and then turned embarrassing.

3 Make a list of adjectives you associate with the event. These are not adjectives that describe you—they are words that describe the event, the setting, or the other people.

4 Make a list of objects you associate with the event. These will all be nouns! List everything that comes to mind. You want the same number of emotions, adjectives, and objects.

5 Randomly circle one word from each list. Put a square around another word from each list. Add parentheses to another word from each list. Keep making random groups of three, one word from each list, until you run out of words. Don't think about the words you are choosing! Use different marks to distinguish the groups.

6 Now write a poem about the event using one group of words—emotion, adjective, noun—in each line. Add verbs and other connecting words to make complete sentences. You might discover you have phrases that make little sense, such as "upset, slow rocks" or "excited, hot dirt." This is a great way to be creative with your images! Copy your final draft into your Poetry Journal.

Words to Know

phenomenon: something that can be observed and studied.

THINK MORE: Did you feel the same emotions while you wrote your poem as you did during the actual event? Did writing about those emotions make you feel differently?

HEALTHY HEARTS

There is some evidence that reciting poetry is healthy for your heart! Researchers in Germany studied the effect of reciting out loud *The Iliad*, an epic by Homer. They discovered that the speakers were unknowingly matching up their heart rates to their breathing rates, which helps control blood pressure. Scientists think that the structure of the poem and the way it requires people to speak when they recite it out loud are responsible for this **phenomenon**.

FREE VERSE!

You've learned a lot about the how and why of poetry, and now it's time to put it all together in a free verse poem. Free verse doesn't rhyme and you don't have to worry about the rhythm. It can be as long or as short as you'd like, just carefully consider each word and how it fits in your poem.

1 Start by choosing an idea. Write about something that's important to you. Use your idea rocks for inspiration if you need to!

2 Line by line, tell the story of your poem. Remember to use literary techniques to make both the meaning and the sounds of the words as clear as possible.

3 After you have completed your first draft, go back and revise. Did you use literary techniques? What is the tone of your poem? Did you maintain this tone all the way through? Revise over and over until you are happy with your poem. This may take several revisions during many weeks.

What did the thief say after getting caught stealing poems?

JUST 4 FUN

I thought it was free verse!

Did you Know?

Poets will sometimes revise poems a hundred times before publishing their works!

4 Copy your poem in your Poetry Journal. Give a poetry reading to family and friends!

REVISION CHECKLIST

Every writer, poets included, revises his or her work many times. The following are some things to check when you revise your work.

* Are all of the words used and spelled correctly?

* Are there any words that could be replaced with more vivid or active ones?

* Is the verb tense correct all the way through? Events in the past should be in past tense (ending in "-ed") and events in the present should be in the present tense.

* Is the tone of the poem consistent?

* Do your similes and metaphors make sense?

* Did you add punctuation in the right places?

* If you are writing a certain form of poetry, do you have the right number of lines or syllables per line? Are the rhyming words in the right places?

* Do you have a title?

READ IT ALOUD!

Hearing poetry read out loud is a very different experience from reading it to yourself. And reading your own poetry out loud is very different from writing it!

1 Choose a poem that you have revised several times already. That way you know it's a good one!

2 Practice alone in your room before going in front of an audience. Every time you speak your words out loud it will get easier to do.

3 Practice in front of a mirror. Try to look at yourself most of the time and only glance at your poem if you really need to. It's best if you can memorize your poem entirely. Be sure to stand up straight and stand still. Don't shift from side to side or stand on one foot or smooth your hair back over and over. These motions will be distracting for your audience!

4 Practice in front of a friend or parent. Make sure you are speaking loudly and clearly. You can never speak too loudly when reading poetry to an audience.

5 It's the big day! Wear something comfortable and bring a glass of water with you to the front of the room. When we're anxious, our mouths can feel dry, and it's very hard to speak with a dry mouth! Read your poem in a loud, clear voice while looking at your audience—and feel good about the applause they give you!

accessible: able to be read and understood by many people.

access: the ability to use or get something.

acrostic poem: a poem where certain letters in each line spell out a word or phrase.

adjective: one of the parts of speech. An adjective is a word, such as *green* or *tall*, that describes a noun or pronoun.

aforetime: in the past.

alliteration: the repetition of a sound at the beginning of two or more neighboring words, such as *zany zebras* or *babbling brook*.

analytical: breaking down problems into small parts to find solutions.

ancient: from a long time ago.

anthology: a collection of poems by different authors.

assonance: the repetition of a vowel sound.

attend: to be present.

audience: a group of people who gather to listen to or watch something.

BCE: put after a date, BCE stands for Before Common Era and counts down to zero. CE stands for Common Era and counts up from zero. These non-religious terms correspond to BC and AD. This book was printed in 2015 CE.

beat: the rhythmic sound in a line of poetry or music.

brainstorm: to think creatively and without judgment.

cadence: the way a person's voice rises and falls while he or she is speaking.

characteristic: a feature of a person, place, or thing.

civilization: a community of people that is advanced in art, science, and government.

cliché: a phrase that is used so often it has lost much of its meaning.

collage: a work of art made up of different pieces of material.

complex: the opposite of simple.

compose: to write.

composition: a piece of music.

concise: giving a lot of information in a few, clear words.

consistent: to stay the same.

consonance: the repetition of a consonant sound.

context: the background or setting of a poem.

contribute: to add to something.

convey: to make an idea understandable.

couplet: two lines of poetry that usually rhyme.

creative: using imagination to come up with new ideas or things.

critically: carefully thinking about what is good or bad about something, or what is right or wrong about it.

deed: an action.

draft: one of several versions of a written piece of work.

dynamic: active or changing, showing a lot of energy or motion.

emotion: a strong feeling about something or someone.

empathy: the ability to share the feelings of others.

emphasize: to give special importance to something.

entrepreneur: a person who takes a risk to start a business.

epic: a long poem, usually about the life of a hero or heroine.

equation: a sentence using mathematical symbols that states two things are the same.

evoke: to bring a picture or feelings to someone's mind.

exaggeration: to say something is much more than it really is.

expertise: special skills or knowledge.

exploit: an adventure.

express: to talk or write about or show in some way something you are thinking or feeling.

foemen: an enemy.

found poem: a poem made up of words found in other writings.

free verse: a poem that doesn't rhyme or follow a regular structure.

galleon: a sailing ship used before the eighteenth century.

generation: all the people born around the same time.

haiku: a short, simple poem that usually has 17 syllables.

haunches: the part of the body above the hip.

hero: a person who can do things that seem impossible.

heroine: a female hero.

hibernate: to sleep through the winter.

Hinduism: the main religion of India. It includes the worship of many gods and the belief that after death you return in a different form.

hurling: throwing.

hyperbole: an exaggerated description.

image: a picture of something.

imagination: the ability to think of something new.

impetuous: done without thought.

innumerable: too many to be counted.

inspiration: something that gives people ideas.

lauds: a song of praise.

limerick: a rhyming poem made up of five lines. The first, second, and fifth lines rhyme with each other, and the third and fourth lines rhyme with each other.

line break: the point at which two lines of text are split.

literary form: a form of writing, such as a story, novel, or poem.

literary journal: a magazine in which poems and stories are published for a small, interested group.

literary techniques: the methods writers use to make their work understandable and interesting.

literature: written work such as poems, plays, and novels.

lyrical: artistically beautiful and expressive.

lyricist: someone who writes the words to a song.

lyrics: the words of a song.

major note: a musical note in the major scale that can sound upbeat.

mechanics: the working parts of something.

melancholy: sadness.

metaphor: a way to describe something by saying it is something else.

minor note: a musical note in the minor scale that can sound sad.

moor: a piece of open land.

murmur: a soft, continuous sound.

mythological: having to do with a myth, which is an ancient story that may or may not be true.

noun: one of the parts of speech. A noun is a word that is the name of something, such as a person, place, or thing.

nursery rhyme: a short poem or song for children that often tells a story.

onomatopoeia: a word that sounds like its meaning.

ordain: to order something.

passage: a journey.

pattern: a way of arranging words in a design to create meaning.

pause: a brief stop or rest.

perfect rhyme: words that have the same ending sound.

personification: to imagine that an object has human or animal characteristics or that an animal has human characteristics.

persuasive: able to get someone to do something.

phase: a period of development.

phenomenon: something that can be observed and studied.

phrase: a group of two or more words that express an idea but do not form a complete sentence.

poem: a piece of writing that describes an event, idea, or emotion in a vivid way.

poet: a person who writes poetry.

poetry: the writings of a poet.

poetry slam: a competition where people perform their poetry for a group of people.

political oppression: when a group, such as the government, treats citizens unfairly.

publish: to produce work for the public.

punctuation mark: a symbol such as a period or a question mark that is used to make writing clear and understandable.

quatrain: four lines of a poem that do not always rhyme.

recite: to speak a poem or other story out loud.

religion: a set of beliefs.

represent: to stand for something.

revision: making a change in something to improve it.

rhyming: when words sound alike except for the first letter.

rhythm: a regular pattern of beats.

rigid: a certain way, not easily changed or unable to bend.

scholar: a person who studies a subject for a long time and knows a lot about it.

shape poem: a poem that forms a shape on the paper.

simile: a figure of speech that compares two different things using the words *like* or *as*.

simplicity: easy to read and understand.

siren: an imaginary woman whose singing made sailors crash their ships.

slant rhyme: words that almost rhyme, such as one and down.

socialized: to do things with other people in a friendly way.

somber: very sad and serious.

specific: clearly defined.

spontaneous: to happen without planning or warning.

stanza: a group of lines that form a part of a poem.

stealthy: quiet, sneaky.

strict: following the rules exactly.

structured: formed with rules and guidelines.

syllable: the separate sounds in a word.

symbol: an image that stands for something else.

sympathy: the feeling that you care about someone else's problems.

tercet: three lines of a poem that do not always rhyme.

text: the words in a piece of writing.

tone: the mood of something.

torrent: a rushing stream of water.

trial: a test.

vaporous: having no solid shape.

verb: one of the parts of speech. A verb is a word, such as *jump* or *see*, that describes an action.

verse: a part of a poem or song.

wheeling: moving in a circular way.

wrath: anger.

wrought: carefully formed.

yea: yes.

POETS

Jack Prelutsky: jackprelutsky.com
Kenn Nesbitt: www.poetry4kids.com
Judith Nicholls: www.poetryarchive.org/poet/judith-nicholls
Judith Viorst: www.poemhunter.com/judith-viorst
John Foster: www.johnfosterchildrenspoet.co.uk
Michael Rosen: www.michaelrosen.co.uk

WEBSITES

Poems and biographies of poets, plus plenty of stuff for kids:
www.poetryfoundation.org

Poems to make you giggle: www.gigglepoetry.com

Children's poetry and information about children's poets:
childrenspoetryarchive.org

Poems, inspiration, and more: www.poetshouse.org

QR CODE GLOSSARY

Page 3: childrenspoetryarchive.org/poet/roald-dahl

Page 14: conjunctions.com/webcon/bervin.htm#

Page 19: tagul.com

Page 21: poets.org/poetsorg/poem/road-not-taken;
pbs.org/wgbh/poetryeverywhere/frost.html

Page 26: world-english.org/english500.htm;
play.magneticpoetry.com/poem/Original/kit/

Page 39: poets.org/poetsorg/poem/do-not-go-gentle-good-night

Page 44: youtube.com/watch?v=usaa6AJFtOE

Page 48: shelsilverstein.com/books/#animations

Page 53: poetryfoundation.org/features/video/7

Page 61: youtube.com/watch?v=qW9oCwpuKDY&feature=kp

Page 63: poets.org/poetsorg/poem/weary-blues

Page 69: incredibox.com; youtube.com/watch?v=Kuw8YjSbKd4&feature=kp

Page 79: etc.usf.edu/lit2go/206/poems-on-various-subjects-religious-and-
moral/4891/an-hymn-to-the-morning

Page 81: poetseers.org/the-great-poets/european-poets/anna-akhmatova-
poems/somewhere-there-is-a-simple-life/index.html